OPENMANUS: BUILD AND AUTOMATE ANYTHING WITH MANUS AI AND OLLAMA

LEANDRO CALADO

The First Practical Guide to
Creating Free, Local AI Agents
Using Open Source Tools

PART I – THE OPENMANUS VISION

1. What Is OpenManus?

OpenManus represents a significant leap forward in accessible artificial intelligence, providing a framework for individuals and developers to harness the power of autonomous AI agents locally and without cost. It is an open-source initiative designed to replicate the capabilities of the groundbreaking Manus AI agent.[1] Unlike traditional AI assistants that often require constant human guidance, OpenManus enables the creation of agents capable of independently planning, executing, and delivering results for complex online tasks.[3]

At its core, OpenManus aims to bridge the gap between conceptualization and execution, allowing users to translate their ideas into tangible outcomes through automated workflows.[6] This is achieved through a modular architecture that allows for the integration of various tools and Large Language Models (LLMs), making it a versatile platform for a wide range of applications.[8] The project emphasizes ease of use and accessibility, aiming to democratize advanced AI agent technology for developers, indie hackers, and AI enthusiasts alike.[1] By leveraging open-source tools like Ollama, OpenManus facilitates the deployment and operation of these intelligent agents on local machines, ensuring privacy, security, and cost-efficiency.[1]

The development of OpenManus was inspired by the need

for an accessible alternative to proprietary AI agents, offering the freedom to modify, extend, and adapt the software to specific project requirements.[9] This open-source nature fosters community collaboration and innovation, allowing users to contribute to the project's growth and benefit from the collective expertise of a diverse group of developers and AI enthusiasts.[2] The ultimate vision of OpenManus is to empower users to build and automate virtually anything, from simple data scraping tasks to complex, multi-step workflows, all within the secure and private confines of their local computing environment.[10]

2. The Rise of Manus AI: China's Autonomous Agent

Manus AI, the inspiration behind OpenManus, emerged as a fully autonomous artificial intelligence agent developed by the Chinese startup company Monica.[3] Officially launched on March 6, 2025, Manus garnered international attention for its ability to independently carry out complex online tasks without direct or continuous human guidance.[3] This marked a significant advancement in AI, moving beyond traditional chatbots that primarily respond to prompts to a system capable of proactive and autonomous action.[6]

The development of Manus was driven by the ambition to create AI agents capable of operating independently, leveraging the power of Large Language Models (LLMs).[4] Its capabilities span a wide range of tasks, including website creation, stock analysis, travel planning, and schedule management.[4] Manus utilizes a multi-agent architecture, combining multiple LLMs such as Anthropic's Claude and Alibaba's Qwen with specialized tools and algorithms to handle different aspects of a task.[6] This allows it to break down complex requests into smaller, manageable steps and execute them systematically.[13]

One of the distinguishing features of Manus is its

computer interface, which provides users with real-time visibility into the agent's actions, offering the ability to intervene if needed.[12] Early reports indicated that Manus excels in research-intensive tasks such as analyzing documents, comparing products, and generating reports.[13] It has also demonstrated strong performance on benchmarks like GAIA, which tests real-world problem-solving skills.[4] While recognized for its advanced capabilities, Manus operates asynchronously in the cloud, allowing tasks to proceed even when the user's device is disconnected.[4] This cloud-based nature, however, contrasts with the local, private approach offered by OpenManus. The emergence of Manus highlighted the increasing potential of autonomous AI agents and spurred the open-source community to develop alternatives like OpenManus, aiming to democratize this powerful technology.[10]

3. Why Ollama Changes the Game (LLMs on Your Laptop)

Ollama is a pivotal open-source tool that significantly alters the landscape of AI development by enabling users to run Large Language Models (LLMs) directly on their local machines.[19] This capability bypasses the traditional reliance on cloud-based APIs for accessing and utilizing LLMs, offering a multitude of advantages in terms of privacy, cost, speed, and control.[19]

By bundling model weights, configuration files, and necessary dependencies into a single package defined by a Modelfile, Ollama simplifies the complexities associated with setting up and running LLMs.[20] It supports a wide array of open-source LLMs, including popular models like Llama 3, Gemma, and Mistral, allowing users to choose the model that best suits their specific needs and hardware capabilities.[23] Once installed, Ollama creates a local API server, allowing applications and tools like OpenManus to interact with the running LLMs seamlessly.[22]

The ability to run LLMs locally with Ollama has profound implications for privacy. Sensitive data processed by the LLM remains on the user's machine, eliminating the risks associated with sending data to third-party cloud servers.[19] This is particularly crucial for users and organizations dealing with confidential information. Furthermore, running LLMs locally can lead to significant cost savings by avoiding the recurring fees associated with cloud-based AI services.[21] Ollama also offers the benefit of faster response times and increased reliability by reducing dependence on external servers and internet connectivity.[19] Finally, it provides users with greater control over the models they use and the ability to customize them for specific tasks.[19] In essence, Ollama empowers users to harness the power of advanced AI directly on their laptops or local servers, paving the way for innovative and private AI applications like those that can be built with OpenManus.

PART II – GETTING STARTED: BUILD YOUR AI STACK

4. Installing Ollama on Mac/Windows/Linux

Setting up Ollama on your system is a straightforward process, designed to get you up and running with local LLMs quickly. Ollama supports macOS, Windows, and Linux, with slightly different installation methods for each platform.[23]

macOS: The easiest way to install Ollama on macOS is by downloading the application directly from the official Ollama website.[29] Simply navigate to ollama.com, click the download button for macOS, and then execute the downloaded .zip file. Drag and drop the Ollama application to your Applications folder. Once installed, you can run Ollama by opening the application. You should see an Ollama icon appear in your system tray, indicating that the server is running in the background.[31]

Windows: Similar to macOS, Windows users can download the Ollama installer from ollama.com.[29] Click the download button for Windows and run the downloaded .exe file. Follow the on-screen instructions to complete the installation. After installation, Ollama will typically start automatically and you'll find its icon in the system tray.[31] If it doesn't start automatically, you can search for "Ollama" in the Start Menu and run it.

Linux: Linux users can install Ollama using a convenient script provided on the website.[23] Open your terminal and run the following command:

```
curl -fsSL https://ollama.com/install.sh | sh
```

This command downloads the installation script and executes it, setting up Ollama on your Linux system. After the script finishes, it's recommended to add your user to the ollama group to avoid permission issues. You can do this with the following commands (replace <username> with your actual username):

```
sudo usermod -aG ollama <username>
newgrp ollama
```

Once Ollama is installed on any of these platforms, you can verify the installation by opening your terminal or command prompt and running the command ollama --version.[28] This should display the installed version of Ollama, confirming that it's ready to use. You can also run ollama list to see any models you might have already downloaded.[28] With Ollama successfully installed, you are now ready to start running local LLMs.

5. Running Local LLMs (Gemma, LLaMA 3, Mistral)

Ollama's primary function is to simplify the process of running Large Language Models (LLMs) locally. It supports a wide variety of open-source models, and downloading and running them is remarkably easy using the Ollama command-line interface (CLI).[23] Here, we will explore how to run some of the popular models like Gemma, LLaMA 3, and Mistral.

Gemma: Gemma is a family of lightweight, open-source models developed by Google DeepMind, inspired by their Gemini models.[23] Ollama makes it very simple to run Gemma. To download and run the default 4B parameter version of Gemma, simply open your terminal or command prompt and type:

```
ollama run gemma
```

Ollama will automatically download the model (if you haven't already) and then provide you with an interactive prompt where you can start asking questions or giving instructions to Gemma.[33] There are also different sizes of Gemma models available, such as 1B, 12B, and 27B parameters. You can specify the size by using a tag, for example, to run the 1B parameter version:

```
ollama run gemma:1b
```

LLaMA 3: LLaMA 3 is the latest generation of open-source large language models from Meta AI, known for its strong performance and instruction-tuned capabilities.[23] To run the default version of LLaMA 3 (typically the 8B parameter instruct model), use the command:

```
ollama run llama3
```

Similar to Gemma, Ollama will handle the download and setup, and then you can start interacting with the model in the terminal. Different variants of LLaMA 3 are also available, often specified with tags indicating parameter size or specific tuning. For example, to run the 3B parameter version:

```
ollama run llama3:3b
```

Mistral: Mistral AI has released several powerful open-source language models, including the Mistral 7B model, which has shown impressive performance across various benchmarks.[23] To run the Mistral 7B model with Ollama, use the command:

```
ollama run mistral
```

Again, Ollama will take care of the downloading and setup process, allowing you to quickly start using the Mistral model.

When you run any of these commands for the first time, Ollama will download the necessary model files, which can take some time depending on your internet connection speed and the size of the model.[22] Subsequent runs will be much faster as the model files will be cached locally.[34] You can use the /bye command or press Ctrl+D to exit the interactive model session.[28] To see a list of all the models you have downloaded, you can use the command ollama list.[28]

6. Setting Up Manus AI: Connecting to Tools & Filesystem

While the original Manus AI is a cloud-based, invite-only platform, OpenManus aims to replicate its functionality locally using open-source tools.[1] Setting up OpenManus typically involves cloning its repository from GitHub and configuring it to connect with the LLMs you want to use via Ollama, as well as any other tools or filesystem access it might need.

The specific setup process can vary depending on the particular OpenManus implementation you are using, as there are several open-source projects aiming to recreate Manus's capabilities.[2] However, the general steps usually involve:

1. **Cloning the Repository:** First, you will need to clone the OpenManus repository from GitHub using git. For example, if you are using the mannaandpoem/OpenManus repository, you would run:

```
git clone https://github.com/mannaandpoem/OpenManus.git
```

```
cd OpenManus
```

2.   **Setting Up the Environment:** OpenManus often requires a specific Python environment with certain dependencies. It's recommended to create a virtual environment using tools like conda or venv and then install the necessary packages using pip.[1] For example:

```
conda create -n open_manus python=3.12
conda activate open_manus
pip install -r requirements.txt
```

3.   **Configuration:** OpenManus typically uses a configuration file (often in toml format, like config.toml) to specify settings such as the LLM to use, API keys (if not using Ollama for local models), and other parameters.[10] If you are planning to use Ollama, you might need to configure OpenManus to point to the local Ollama server, which usually runs at http://localhost:11434.[54] Some OpenManus implementations are designed to work with local models via Ollama without requiring API keys.[1] You may need to edit the configuration file to specify the model names you have downloaded with Ollama (e.g., llama3, gemma, mistral).

4.   **Connecting to Tools and Filesystem:** OpenManus's ability to automate tasks often relies on its integration with various tools, such as web browsers, code editors, and the local filesystem.[4] The way OpenManus connects to these tools depends on its specific design. Some implementations might use libraries like Selenium or Playwright for browser automation [50], while others might have built-in functionalities or require specific configurations to interact with the filesystem. You might need to ensure that any

required drivers or dependencies for these tools are installed on your system.

The documentation for the specific OpenManus project you are using will provide detailed instructions on these steps and any additional configurations required. Once set up, OpenManus can leverage the local LLMs running via Ollama to perform a wide range of automated tasks.

7. Creating Your First OpenManus Agent (Planning + Execution)

With Ollama and OpenManus installed and configured, you are now ready to create your first autonomous AI agent. The core of an OpenManus agent lies in its ability to plan a sequence of actions and then execute those actions to achieve a desired goal.[5] This involves breaking down a complex task into smaller, manageable steps and utilizing various tools to carry out each step.

The process of creating an agent with OpenManus typically involves the following stages:

1. **Defining the Objective:** First, you need to clearly define what you want your agent to accomplish. This could be anything from fetching specific information from the web to generating a report or automating a series of tasks on your computer. The more specific your objective, the better the agent will be able to plan and execute.

2. **Prompting OpenManus:** You interact with OpenManus by providing it with a natural language prompt that describes your objective.[12] This prompt serves as the initial instruction for the agent. For example, you might prompt: "Find the current price of Bitcoin and the latest news about it."

3. **Planning:** Upon receiving your prompt, OpenManus, powered by the underlying LLM (running via Ollama), will analyze the request and formulate a plan to achieve the objective.[5] This plan consists of a series of steps that the agent will take. In our Bitcoin example, the plan might involve steps like:

    o   Use a web browser tool to search for the current price of

Bitcoin.
- Extract the price from the search results.
- Use a web browser tool to search for the latest news about Bitcoin.
- Identify and summarize the key news articles.
- Present the price and news summary to the user.

4. **Execution:** Once the plan is created, OpenManus will begin executing each step in the plan.[5] This often involves using various tools that OpenManus has access to, such as a web browser tool (to perform searches and interact with web pages), a code execution tool (to run Python scripts for data analysis or other tasks), or a file system tool (to read or write files). The agent will interact with these tools based on the instructions generated in the planning phase.

5. **Observation and Iteration:** As the agent executes each step, it observes the results and uses this information to proceed with the next steps in the plan.[6] If a step fails or doesn't produce the desired outcome, the agent might revise its plan or try a different approach. This iterative process allows the agent to handle unexpected issues and work towards the final objective autonomously.

6. **Output:** Finally, once the agent has completed all the steps in its plan, it will provide you with the result, which could be the information you requested, a generated report, or the completion of the automated tasks.[5] In our Bitcoin example, the agent would present the current price and a summary of the latest news.

To run your first OpenManus agent, you will typically execute a Python script from the OpenManus repository in your terminal.[1] The exact command might vary depending on the specific implementation, but it often looks something like:

```
python main.py
```

After running this command, you will likely be prompted in the terminal to enter your idea or task. For example:

What would you like OpenManus to do?

You would then type your prompt and press Enter. OpenManus will then start the planning and execution process, and you will usually see output in the terminal indicating the steps the agent is taking.[13] For instance, if you asked for the weather in London, you might see the agent indicating that it is using a browser tool to search for weather information and then extracting the relevant data.

The ability of OpenManus to break down complex requests into smaller, manageable steps [7] is a core feature of autonomous agents, enabling them to handle intricate workflows without constant human intervention. Unlike traditional AI models that might respond directly to a prompt, autonomous agents like those built with OpenManus can reason through a problem by creating a plan of action. This involves identifying the necessary steps to achieve the user's goal, selecting appropriate tools or sub-agents for each step, and then executing those steps sequentially. This planning capability allows the agent to handle tasks that require multiple stages or involve dependencies between different actions.

The visualization of the agent's thought process [12] in OpenManus provides transparency and allows users to understand how the agent is working towards the solution. Many AI systems operate as "black boxes," where the reasoning behind their outputs is not readily apparent. OpenManus, as suggested by the references to Manus AI's real-time interface, aims to provide a more transparent experience. By showing the steps the agent is taking, the tools it's using, and its intermediate thoughts, OpenManus allows users to understand the agent's decision-making process. This transparency is crucial for building trust in the AI and for enabling users to identify and debug any issues that might arise during the agent's execution.

PART III – REAL PROJECTS: BUILD & SCRAPE ANYTHING

8. Project 1: Create a Stock Dashboard with AI + Python

This project will guide you through building an AI-powered stock dashboard using OpenManus, Ollama, and Python. The dashboard will automatically fetch stock data, analyze it using a local LLM, and visualize the results.

1.   **Fetching Stock Data:** OpenManus can be instructed to fetch stock data using Python libraries like yfinance.[58] The agent can be prompted to write and execute Python code using a CodeAgent or a similar tool within OpenManus to achieve this. Here's an example of how to get historical stock data for a ticker symbol using yfinance:

```python
import yfinance as yf
import pandas as pd

# Define the ticker symbol
ticker_symbol = "AAPL"

# Define the time period
start_date = "2024-11-01"
end_date = "2024-11-07"

# Fetch the histrical data
stock_data = yf.download(ticker_symbol, start=start_date, end=end_date)
```

```
# Print the data
print(stock_data)

# Save to CSV (optional)
stock_data.to_csv("aapl_stock_data.csv")
```

The OpenManus agent can be instructed to generate and run this code snippet.

2. **Analyzing Stock Data with Ollama:** Once the data is fetched, OpenManus can send prompts to Ollama (running locally via its API) to analyze it. You can instruct the agent to perform tasks like calculating moving averages, identifying support and resistance levels, or summarizing news sentiment related

   to the stock. Snippets [4] highlight Manus AI's capabilities in financial analysis and dashboard creation, which OpenManus aims to replicate. For example, you could prompt Ollama with the stock data to identify any significant trends or patterns.

3. **Data Visualization:** Python libraries like plotly or streamlit

   can be used to visualize the stock data.[58] Here's an example using plotly to create a basic candlestick chart:

```
import plotly.graph_objects as go
import pandas as pd

# Load the stock data from CSV (assuming it was saved)
data = pd.read_csv("aapl_stock_data.csv", index_col='Date')

# Create the candlestick chart
fig = go.Figure(data=[go.Candlestick(x=data.index,
        open=data['Open'],
        high=data['High'],
        low=data['Low'],
        close=data['Close'])])
```

```
fig.update_layout(title='AAPL Stock Price',
        xaxis_title='Date',
        yaxis_title='Price')

fig.show()
```

OpenManus can be instructed to generate and run this code to display the chart.

4.   **Integration with OpenManus:** To integrate these components, you would instruct OpenManus to:
   o   Fetch the stock data using the Python code.
   o   Send the data to Ollama for analysis with specific prompts.
   o   Generate the visualization using the Python code.
   o   Potentially display the chart using streamlit to create a simple web-based dashboard.[58]

5.   **Automation:** To automatically update the dashboard, you can schedule the OpenManus script to run periodically using system tools like cron (on Linux/macOS) or Task Scheduler (on Windows).

This project demonstrates a practical application of combining OpenManus, Ollama, and Python for real-time data analysis and visualization, showcasing the power of local AI for financial insights. By integrating different open-source tools, this project illustrates how to build a sophisticated application locally. OpenManus acts as the orchestrator, managing the workflow of fetching data, using Ollama for AI-powered analysis (like identifying patterns or sentiment), and leveraging Python libraries for visualization. This showcases the potential of local AI to provide personalized financial insights without relying on cloud-based services or proprietary software.

Table 2: Example Stock Data

Date	Open	High	Low	Close	Volume

2024-11-01	150.00	152.50	149.00	152.00	1,000,000
2024-11-02	152.00	153.00	151.50	152.50	800,000
2024-11-03	152.50	154.00	152.00	153.50	1,200,000
2024-11-04	153.50	155.00	153.00	154.50	950,000
2024-11-05	154.50	156.00	154.00	155.50	1,100,000
2024-11-06	155.50	157.00	155.00	156.50	1,050,000
2024-11-07	156.50	158.00	156.00	157.00	1,300,000

This table shows sample historical stock data that can be fetched using yfinance. The 'AI Analysis Results' mentioned in Snippet [58] would then interpret this data, possibly identifying trends like an upward trend based on the increasing closing prices. The dashboard would visually represent this data using candlestick charts or other relevant visualizations.

9. Project 2: Automate a Full SEO Audit from Scratch

This project demonstrates how to automate a comprehensive SEO audit of a website using OpenManus and local LLMs via Ollama. This process involves crawling the website, analyzing its content for SEO factors, and generating a report.

1. **Website Crawling:** OpenManus can utilize browser automation tools like Selenium or Playwright [50] to crawl a website. You can instruct the agent to use a BrowserUseTool [50] to navigate through the website's pages. For example, you might provide OpenManus with a starting URL and instruct it to follow all the links within the domain.

```
from browser_use import Agent, BrowserConfig
from ollama import LocalLLM
```

```python
class SEOCrawler:
    def __init__(self):
        self.config = BrowserConfig(headless=True)
        self.agent = Agent(task="SEO Audit Crawler",
config=self.config)

    async def crawl_site(self, start_url):
        # Initialize URL queue and visited set
        urls_to_visit = {start_url}
        visited_urls = set()

        # Configure browser automation
        await self.agent.setup_browser()

        while urls_to_visit:
            current_url = urls_to_visit.pop()
            if current_url in visited_urls:
                continue

            # Navigate to URL and extract content
            await self.agent.navigate(current_url)
            html_content = await self.agent.get_page_source()

            # Extract links for next iteration
            new_urls = await self._extract_links(html_content)
            urls_to_visit.update(new_urls)

            yield current_url, html_content

            visited_urls.add(current_url)
```

2. **Content Analysis with Ollama:** Once the website content is crawled, OpenManus can use Ollama to analyze it for SEO

ranking factors.[1] The agent can send the HTML content of each page to Ollama with prompts like:

o   "Analyze this HTML for the presence and quality of meta descriptions and title tags."

o   "Identify the main keywords used on this page."

o   "Check for the presence of appropriate heading tags (H1, H2, etc.)."

o   "Look for any broken links on this page."

o   "Assess the loading speed of this page based on the provided information (if available)."

OpenManus can be configured to iterate through each crawled page and send these analysis prompts to Ollama.

```python
class SEOAnalyzer:
    def __init__(self):
        self.llm = LocalLLM()


    async def analyze_page(self, url, html_content):
        # Define SEO analysis prompts
        prompts = [
            {
                'prompt': f"Analyze the meta description and title tags in this HTML: {html_content}",
                'analysis_type': 'meta_tags'
            },
            {
                'prompt': f"Identify main keywords and their density in this content: {html_content}",
                'analysis_type': 'keyword_analysis'
            },
            {
                'prompt': f"Check heading structure (H1-H6) in this HTML: {html_content}",
                'analysis_type': 'heading_structure'
            }
        ]
```

```
# Process each prompt
findings = []
for prompt in prompts:
    response = await self.llm.query(prompt['prompt'])
    findings.append({
        'url': url,
        'analysis_type': prompt['analysis_type'],
        'results': response
    })

return findings
```

3.   **SEO Ranking Factor Identification:** By analyzing the responses from Ollama, OpenManus can identify key SEO elements and potential issues. For instance, if Ollama reports missing meta descriptions or title tags, or a high density of certain keywords, OpenManus can flag these as areas for improvement. Similarly, if Ollama detects broken links or suggests slow loading times, these would be noted as technical SEO errors.

4.   **Report Compilation:** Finally, OpenManus can compile an actionable SEO optimization report. This could involve writing the findings to a local file (e.g., a text file or a CSV file) or displaying the report in the terminal. The report could be structured into sections such as:

o   **Keyword Analysis:** Listing the main keywords found on the site and their density.

o   **On-Page Optimization:** Suggestions for improving meta descriptions, title tags, and heading tag usage.

o   **Technical SEO Issues:** Reporting any broken links or potential slow loading times.

```
import json
from datetime import datetime

class SEOReporter:
    def __init__(self):
```

```
    self.report_data = {}

def compile_report(self, findings):
    report_date = datetime.now().strftime("%Y-%m-%d %H:%M:
%S")

    # Organize findings by category
    self.report_data = {
        'audit_date': report_date,
        'pages_analyzed': len(findings),
        'meta_tags_issues': [],
        'keyword_analysis': {},
        'heading_structure': {}
    }

    # Process findings
    for finding in findings:
        if finding['analysis_type'] == 'meta_tags':
            self._process_meta_tags(finding)
        elif finding['analysis_type'] == 'keyword_analysis':
            self._process_keywords(finding)
        elif finding['analysis_type'] == 'heading_structure':
            self._process_headings(finding)

    return self.report_data

def generate_report_file(self,
filename='seo_audit_report.json'):
    with open(filename, 'w') as f:
        json.dump(self.report_data, f, indent=2)
```

5. **Prompt Guidance:** Effective prompts are crucial for guiding Ollama in identifying key SEO elements. For example, you can prompt Ollama with specific instructions to extract title tags using a prompt like: "Extract the content within the <title> tags from the following HTML." Similarly, for meta descriptions: "Extract the content of the meta tag with the

name 'description' from the following HTML."

This project showcases the potential of local AI agents to automate complex web analysis tasks, providing valuable insights for website optimization without relying on expensive third-party tools. Automating SEO audits can save significant time and effort for website owners and marketers. By using OpenManus to handle the crawling and Ollama to perform the analysis, this project demonstrates a cost-effective and potentially more private way to conduct these audits locally. This eliminates the need to share website data with external SEO audit services.

10. Project 3: Build a Self-Updating Daily Report Generator

This project guides you through creating an OpenManus agent that automatically generates daily reports based on specified data sources, leveraging the capabilities of local LLMs via Ollama.

Setting Up OpenManus with Ollama

First, configure OpenManus to work with Ollama as your local LLM provider

```
[llm]
model = "qwq"
base_url = "http://ollamahost:11434/v1"
max_tokens = 4096
temperature = 0.0
```

1. **Data Source Configuration:** First, you need to configure your OpenManus agent to access the data sources you want to include in your daily report. This could involve fetching data from various APIs using the requests library, reading from local CSV or JSON files, or connecting to databases using appropriate Python connectors. The OpenManus agent can be instructed to use different tools or even write and execute Python code to retrieve this data.

2. **Data Retrieval:** Once configured, the OpenManus agent can be scheduled to automatically fetch the latest data from these sources at a определенное время each day. For example,

it could retrieve the previous day's sales figures from a database, the latest news headlines from an API, or project task completion data from a local file.

3.   **Data Processing and Summarization with Ollama:** After retrieving the raw data, OpenManus can use Ollama to process it, summarize key information, and format it into a report.[4] The agent can send the raw data to Ollama with prompts like:

o   For sales data: "Summarize the total sales, top-selling products, and any significant trends from yesterday's sales data."

o   For news headlines: "Generate a concise daily news briefing summarizing the top headlines across different categories."

o   For project updates: "Based on the task completion data, provide a summary of the progress made yesterday and any potential roadblocks."

```
data_sources:
 sales_db:
  type: database
  connector: mysql
  host: localhost
  port: 3306
  database: sales_db
  query: "SELECT * FROM daily_sales WHERE date =
DATE_SUB(CURRENT_DATE, INTERVAL 1 DAY)"

 news_api:
  type: api
  url: https://news-api.example.com/headlines
  auth_token: your_api_key
  params:
   category: business
   limit: 10

 project_data:
  type: file
  path: /path/to/project/data.csv
  format: csv
```

4. **Report Generation:** Based on the summarized information from Ollama, OpenManus can format the report into a readable format. This could involve creating a plain text report, a Markdown file, or even using Python libraries to generate more structured reports (e.g., in HTML or PDF format).

```python
from datetime import datetime
import yaml
import os

class DailyReportGenerator:
    def __init__(self, config_path):
        self.config = self._load_config(config_path)
        self.openmanus = OpenManusAgent()


    def _load_config(self, path):
        with open(path, 'r') as f:
            return yaml.safe_load(f)


    def fetch_data(self):
        """Fetch data from configured sources"""
        data = {}
        for source_name, config in self.config['data_sources'].items():
            if config['type'] == 'database':
                data[source_name] = self._fetch_from_database(config)
            elif config['type'] == 'api':
                data[source_name] = self._fetch_from_api(config)
            elif config['type'] == 'file':
                data[source_name] = self._read_file(config)
        return data


    def _process_with_ollama(self, data):
        """Process raw data using Ollama"""
        processed_data = {}
```

```python
    for section, content in data.items():
        prompt = self._generate_prompt(section, content)
        processed_data[section] =
self.openmanus.query(prompt)
    return processed_data


def generate_report(self):
    """Main report generation function"""
    raw_data = self.fetch_data()
    processed_data = self._process_with_ollama(raw_data)
    report_content = self._format_report(processed_data)
    self._save_report(report_content)

def _generate_prompt(self, section, data):
    """Generate Ollama prompt based on data type"""
    prompts = {
        'sales': "Analyze the sales data and provide insights on
trends, top performers, and revenue metrics.",
        'news': "Summarize the news headlines into a concise
daily briefing.",
        'projects': "Generate a progress report based on the
project data."
    }
    return prompts.get(section, "Provide a detailed analysis
of the provided data.")
```

5. **Scheduling Automation:** To make the report generation fully automatic, you can use system scheduling tools to run the OpenManus script at a определенное время each day.[35] On Linux or macOS, you can use cron to schedule the script. On Windows, the Task Scheduler can be used for this purpose.

```
# Edit crontab
crontab -e

# Add daily schedule (runs at 8 AM every day)
0 8 * * * python /path/to/report_generator.py
```

Examples of different types of daily reports that can be generated include:

- **Sales Reports:** Summarizing daily sales, revenue, top-performing products, and customer trends.
- **News Summaries:** Compiling the most important news stories from various sources.
- **Project Updates:** Reporting on the progress of tasks, milestones achieved, and any delays in projects.
- **Financial Market Briefings:** Summarizing the day's key market movements, stock performance, and economic news.

This project illustrates how local AI agents can automate routine information gathering and reporting tasks, freeing up valuable time for more strategic activities. Many professionals spend a significant amount of time each day compiling reports from various data sources. By automating this process with OpenManus and Ollama, users can have these reports generated automatically, saving time and ensuring consistency. The local nature of this setup also means sensitive data doesn't need to be shared with external services.

11. Project 4: Scrape, Clean, and Visualize Web Data Locally

This project demonstrates how to build an OpenManus agent that can autonomously scrape data from websites, clean it, and generate visualizations, all within your local environment using Ollama and Python.

1. **Web Scraping with OpenManus:** You can instruct OpenManus to use browser automation tools like Selenium or Playwright (via a BrowserUseTool) to extract data from web pages.[50] The agent can be given a target URL and instructions on which elements to extract (e.g., data from tables, lists, or specific HTML elements).[47]
2. **Data Cleaning with Python:** Once the data is scraped, it often needs to be cleaned and preprocessed before analysis

and visualization. OpenManus can be instructed to write and execute Python code using libraries like Pandas to perform these tasks. Common data cleaning techniques include:

- o **Removing duplicates:** Identifying and removing identical rows in the dataset.
- o **Handling missing values:** Filling in missing data or removing rows with missing values.
- o **Data type conversion:** Ensuring that data is in the correct format (e.g., converting strings to numbers or dates).
- o **Text processing:** Cleaning up text data by removing special characters, extra spaces, or converting to lowercase.

3. **Assistance from Ollama:** Ollama can be used to understand the scraped data and potentially assist in the cleaning process.[11] For example, you could prompt Ollama with a sample of the data and ask it to identify any outliers or inconsistencies. Ollama's understanding of natural language can also be helpful in interpreting and cleaning text-based data.

4. **Data Visualization with Python:** After cleaning the data, OpenManus can use Python visualization libraries like Matplotlib or Seaborn to generate various types of plots.[15] Depending on the nature of the data, you might create:

- o **Bar charts:** To compare categorical data.
- o **Scatter plots:** To explore relationships between two numerical variables.
- o **Line graphs:** To show trends over time.
- o **Histograms:** To visualize the distribution of a single numerical variable.

OpenManus can be instructed to generate the necessary Python code to create these visualizations based on the cleaned data.

5. **Workflow Integration:** The entire workflow – scraping, cleaning, and visualizing – can be orchestrated by the OpenManus agent. You would provide an initial prompt specifying the website to scrape and the type of visualization

you want to generate. OpenManus would then plan and execute the necessary steps, leveraging browser automation, Python code execution, and the analytical capabilities of Ollama.

Based on the previous discussion about web scraping, data cleaning, and visualization, here's how to implement it in Python:

Basic Implementation

First, install the necessary packages:

```
pip install selenium pandas matplotlib seaborn
beautifulsoup4 requests
```

Here's a basic implementation that combines all three components:

```python
from selenium import webdriver
import pandas as pd
import matplotlib.pyplot as plt
import seaborn as sns
from bs4 import BeautifulSoup
import time

def scrape_website(url):
    # Initialize browser
    driver = webdriver.Chrome()
    driver.get(url)

    # Wait for page load
    time.sleep(2)

    # Parse HTML content
    soup = BeautifulSoup(driver.page_source, 'html.parser')
    driver.quit()

    return soup
```

```python
def clean_data(data):
    df = pd.DataFrame(data)

    # Remove duplicates
    df = df.drop_duplicates()

    # Handle missing values
    df = df.fillna(df.mean())

    # Convert data types
    numeric_cols = ['price', 'quantity']  # Adjust column names
as needed
    df[numeric_cols] = df[numeric_cols].apply(pd.to_numeric,
errors='coerce')

    return df

def visualize_data(df):
    plt.figure(figsize=(12, 6))

    # Create side-by-side plots
    plt.subplot(1, 2, 1)
    sns.barplot(x='category', y='value', data=df)

    plt.subplot(1, 2, 2)
    sns.scatterplot(x='x_axis', y='y_axis', data=df)

    plt.tight_layout()
    plt.savefig('visualization.png')

# Example usage
url = "your_target_url.com"
soup = scrape_website(url)

# Extract specific data (example)
```

```
data = []
for item in soup.find_all('div', class_='item'):
  data.append({
    'name': item.find('h2').text.strip(),
    'price': item.find('span', class_='price').text.strip(),
    'category': item.find('span', class_='category').text.strip()
  })

df = clean_data(data)
visualize_data(df)
```

Advanced Implementation with Error Handling

```
import logging
from selenium.webdriver.support.ui import WebDriverWait
from selenium.webdriver.support import
expected_conditions as EC
from selenium.common.exceptions import
TimeoutException, NoSuchElementException

class WebScraper:
  def __init__(self):
    self.driver = None
    logging.basicConfig(level=logging.INFO)

  def initialize_driver(self):
    try:
      self.driver = webdriver.Chrome()
      return True
    except Exception as e:
      logging.error(f"Failed to initialize driver: {str(e)}")
      return False

  def scrape_data(self, url, timeout=30):
    try:
      self.driver.get(url)
      element = WebDriverWait(self.driver, timeout).until(
        EC.presence_of_element_located(('css selector',
'.content'))
```

```
    )

    soup =
BeautifulSoup(element.get_attribute('outerHTML'),
'html.parser')
        return soup
    except TimeoutException:
        logging.warning(f"Timeout waiting for page load:
{url}")
        return None
    except Exception as e:
        logging.error(f"Scraping failed: {str(e)}")
        return None


  def cleanup(self):
    if self.driver:
      self.driver.quit()

def main():
  scraper = WebScraper()
  if not scraper.initialize_driver():
    return


  try:
    # Replace with actual URL and selectors
    url = "your_target_url.com"
    soup = scraper.scrape_data(url)


    if soup:
      df = clean_data(extract_data_from_soup(soup))
      visualize_data(df)


  finally:
    scraper.cleanup()
```

This project combines web scraping, data processing, and

visualization using local AI tools, showcasing a complete data analysis workflow that prioritizes privacy and cost-efficiency. This demonstrates a full end-to-end data pipeline that can be run entirely locally. By using OpenManus to automate the scraping, Python/Pandas for cleaning, Ollama for potential analysis and cleaning assistance, and visualization libraries for presenting the data, users can perform comprehensive data analysis without relying on cloud-based platforms or sharing their data with external services.

12. Bonus: Voice-Controlled AI Assistant (Offline)

This bonus project explores the exciting possibility of creating a fully offline voice-controlled AI assistant using OpenManus and Ollama, offering a high degree of privacy and independence from internet connectivity.

1.   **Voice Recognition:** To enable voice control, you can integrate open-source voice recognition libraries like Vosk or CMU Sphinx with OpenManus. These libraries can transcribe spoken audio into text. This would likely involve developing custom tools or agents within OpenManus that can interact with these libraries to capture audio from your microphone and convert it into a textual format.

2.   **Natural Language Understanding with Ollama:** Once the voice input is transcribed into text, this text will serve as the prompt for Ollama, which will handle the natural language understanding and generate an appropriate response.[13] Since Ollama runs locally, this entire process remains offline and private.

3.   **Text-to-Speech:** To provide spoken output from Ollama's responses, you can integrate open-source text-to-speech (TTS) libraries such as eSpeak or MaryTTS. Similar to voice recognition, this would require creating custom tools within OpenManus that can take the text response from Ollama and use the TTS engine to generate spoken audio. Snippets [66] and [63] provide some context on text-to-speech functionality in

similar projects.

4. **Combining the Components:** A basic outline for creating this offline voice assistant could involve the following steps in a continuous loop:

   o **Listen for Audio Input:** Use the voice recognition library to continuously listen for spoken commands.

   o **Transcribe Audio to Text:** Once speech is detected, transcribe it into a text prompt.

   o **Send Prompt to Ollama via OpenManus:** Pass the transcribed text as a prompt to the local Ollama server through OpenManus.

   o **Receive Text Response from Ollama:** OpenManus receives the generated text response from Ollama.

   o **Convert Text to Speech:** Use the text-to-speech library to convert the text response into spoken audio.

   o **Play Spoken Response:** Output the generated audio through your computer's speakers.

Snippet [63] provides a good overview of the tech stack involved in a similar project, using Whisper for transcription, Ollama with Llama-2 for the LLM, and Bark for TTS. While Whisper and Bark are also open-source, Vosk and eSpeak offer lightweight alternatives that might be more suitable for a fully offline setup.

This bonus project explores a more advanced application of local AI, demonstrating the potential for building fully offline and private voice assistants. Creating a voice assistant that operates entirely offline addresses significant privacy concerns associated with cloud-based assistants. By combining open-source tools for speech recognition, natural language processing (via Ollama), and text-to-speech, this project showcases the feasibility of building such a system locally, giving users complete control over their data and interactions.

PART IV – BEYOND BASICS

13. Multi-Agent Systems with OpenManus

The concept of multi-agent systems (MAS) involves multiple autonomous AI agents working collaboratively to solve complex tasks that would be difficult for a single agent to handle.[2] OpenManus's design, inspired by the original Manus AI, inherently supports the creation of such systems through its modular architecture.[2]

Within OpenManus, different types of agents can be defined, each with specialized roles and capabilities. Examples include a Project Manager agent that understands user needs and manages the overall execution, a PlanningAgent that breaks down complex tasks into actionable steps, and ToolCallAgent or ExecutionAgent that handle specific AI-powered operations by interacting with various tools.[8]

To orchestrate these agents within OpenManus, you can configure them to work together in a coordinated manner. For instance, when faced with a complex user request, the Project Manager agent could first engage the PlanningAgent to develop a detailed plan. This plan would then be divided into sub-tasks, which are delegated to specialized ToolCallAgents. These agents would then utilize the appropriate tools – perhaps a web browser agent to gather information, a code execution agent to run necessary scripts, or a file system agent to manage local files – to complete their assigned sub-tasks. The results from these individual agents would then be collected and synthesized by the Project Manager to provide a comprehensive solution to the user's initial request.

The benefits of using a multi-agent system like this are numerous. It can lead to increased efficiency by allowing tasks to be performed in parallel by different agents. It also enhances robustness, as the system can potentially continue functioning even if one agent encounters an issue, with other agents possibly compensating or taking over. Furthermore, MAS enables the tackling of more complex workflows that require a diverse set of expertise and capabilities, with each specialized agent contributing its unique strengths to the overall solution. The modular design of OpenManus makes it relatively straightforward to define new types of agents and configure their interactions, allowing for the creation of highly sophisticated and adaptable autonomous AI systems.

14. Security, Sandboxing, and Safe Local Executions

When working with local AI agents, especially those that can execute code or interact with external tools and the filesystem, security becomes a paramount concern.[67] It is crucial to ensure that the agent's activities do not inadvertently harm your system or compromise your data. This is where the concept of sandboxing comes into play.

Sandboxing involves creating an isolated environment for the AI agent to operate in, preventing it from accessing or affecting the host system or other applications in unintended ways.[67] Several sandboxing techniques can be employed with OpenManus and Ollama. For instance, when OpenManus needs to execute code (perhaps generated by the LLM for data analysis or automation), it is highly recommended to do so within a containerized environment using Docker.[67] Docker allows you to define lightweight, isolated containers that include only the necessary software and dependencies for the code to run, limiting its access to the rest of your system.

For tasks involving browser automation, which is often used for web scraping or interacting with web applications, modern web browsers themselves provide a level of sandboxing for the web pages and scripts they run.[68] However, it's still important to be mindful of the permissions granted to the browser automation tools used by OpenManus.

To ensure safe local execution of AI agents, it's essential to follow some best practices. One key principle is to limit the agent's access to sensitive files and network resources as much as possible. This can be achieved through careful configuration of file system permissions and network access controls within the sandboxed environment. The principle of least privilege should be applied, granting the agent only the minimum permissions necessary to perform its intended tasks. Regularly reviewing the agent's activities and any logs it produces can also help in identifying and addressing potential security issues. By implementing robust sandboxing and adhering to security best practices, you can significantly mitigate the risks associated with running autonomous AI agents locally.

15. Deploying OpenManus on Raspberry Pi or Mini-PCs

Deploying OpenManus and Ollama on resource-constrained devices like Raspberry Pi or mini-PCs opens up exciting possibilities for running AI agents in edge computing scenarios.[45] These devices offer a cost-effective and energy-efficient way to bring localized AI capabilities to various applications.

However, it's important to be aware of the hardware requirements and limitations when running LLMs on such devices. A Raspberry Pi 5 with at least 8GB of RAM (16GB is often recommended for better performance) is generally considered a suitable platform for running smaller language models.[71] Adequate storage space (at least 32GB microSD card) and proper cooling are also crucial for stable operation.[71]

Installing Ollama on a Raspberry Pi is typically straightforward using the same installation script as for other Linux systems [76]:

```
curl -fsSL https://ollama.com/install.sh | sh
```

You might encounter some issues, such as the automatic detection of GPUs [79], as Raspberry Pis often don't have dedicated NVIDIA or AMD GPUs. However, Ollama can still run on the CPU, albeit with slower performance. It's also important to ensure you are using a 64-bit operating system on your Raspberry Pi for compatibility.[76]

To optimize OpenManus for lower resource usage on these devices, consider using smaller language models with Ollama (e.g., models with fewer parameters). You might also need to reduce the complexity of the tasks you assign to the agent. Additionally, you could explore optimizing the OpenManus code itself for better performance on resource-constrained hardware.

Deploying local AI agents on edge devices like Raspberry Pis can enable a wide range of interesting use cases, such as smart home automation systems that process voice commands locally for enhanced privacy, environmental monitoring stations that perform real-time analysis of sensor data, or personal assistants that operate entirely offline. While the performance might not match that of more powerful desktop systems, the ability to run private and localized AI solutions on these small devices presents a compelling opportunity for various applications.

PART V – RESOURCES

16. Best Open Source Tools to Combine with OpenManus

To maximize the potential of OpenManus, you can integrate it with a variety of other open-source tools. Here are some of the best options:

- **Code Editors:**
  - **VSCode** [9]: A highly popular and extensible code editor with excellent support for Python and JavaScript, making it ideal for developing and debugging OpenManus agents. Its integration capabilities allow for seamless workflow management.
  - **Atom:** A customizable and open-source text editor that's also well-suited for coding in Python and JavaScript, offering a range of packages to enhance functionality.
  - **Sublime Text:** While not strictly open-source, Sublime Text has a generous free trial and is a powerful and lightweight editor favored by many developers for its speed and features.
- **Web Browsers:**
  - **Chromium:** The open-source project behind Google Chrome, Chromium is a powerful and versatile browser that can be automated using tools like Selenium and Playwright for web scraping and agent interaction with web applications.
  - **Firefox:** Another excellent open-source browser with robust developer tools and automation capabilities, making it a great choice for tasks involving web interaction within OpenManus.
- **Terminal Applications:**

- o **Bash:** The default shell on most Linux and macOS systems, Bash is essential for running OpenManus scripts and interacting with Ollama via the command line.
- o **Zsh:** An alternative shell that offers many enhancements over Bash, including improved tab completion and customization options, making it a favorite among developers.
- o **PowerShell:** The command-line shell for Windows, PowerShell provides a powerful way to interact with the operating system and run OpenManus scripts on Windows.
- **Python Libraries:**
  - o **requests:** A library for making HTTP requests, crucial for OpenManus agents that need to interact with APIs to fetch data or trigger actions.
  - o **beautifulsoup4:** A library for parsing HTML and XML documents, often used in conjunction with web scraping tools to extract specific information from web pages.
  - o **selenium** and **playwright:** Powerful libraries for automating web browsers, allowing OpenManus agents to navigate websites, interact with elements, and extract data programmatically.
  - o **pandas:** A library providing data structures and tools for data analysis, essential for cleaning, manipulating, and analyzing data scraped from the web or obtained from other sources.
  - o **numpy:** A fundamental library for numerical computing in Python, often used in conjunction with pandas for more advanced data analysis tasks.
  - o **matplotlib** and **seaborn:** Libraries for creating static, interactive, and animated visualizations in Python, allowing you to generate charts and graphs from data processed by OpenManus agents.
  - o **streamlit** and **gradio:** Libraries for quickly building interactive web interfaces for your Python scripts, enabling you to create simple dashboards or demo applications for your OpenManus agents.

- o **langchain** and **llama-index:** Frameworks for building applications powered by large language models, which can be integrated with OpenManus to create more sophisticated agent workflows and retrieval-augmented generation (RAG) capabilities.

- o **ollama-python** [36]: A Python client library for interacting with the Ollama API, allowing OpenManus agents to easily send prompts to and receive responses from locally running LLMs.

- o **Dolphin MCP** [82]: A Python library and CLI tool that simplifies the integration of various language models like Ollama and OpenAI, as well as external data sources, into a unified workflow.

17. Prompt Libraries and Agent Templates

To help you get started with building your own AI agents using OpenManus and Ollama, having access to effective prompt libraries and agent templates can be incredibly beneficial.

For interacting with LLMs via Ollama, consider these example prompts categorized by use case:

- **Data Analysis:**
  - o "Summarize the key trends in this dataset: [insert your data here]"
  - o "Identify any correlations between [variable 1] and [variable 2] in the following data: [insert your data here]"
  - o "Based on this text: [insert text], what are the main arguments for and against [topic]?"
- **Web Scraping Instructions for OpenManus:**
  - o "Go to and extract all the product names and prices from the product listings."
  - o "Navigate to and follow all the links on the page. For each linked page, extract the main title and the first paragraph."
  - o "Visit and find the contact email address listed on the site."
- **Content Generation Prompts:**

- o "Write a short blog post about the benefits of using local AI agents."
- o "Generate a product description for a new open-source AI tool."
- o "Create a tweet announcing the release of OpenManus."

When using these prompts, remember to tailor them to the specific LLM you are using (Gemma, LLaMA 3, Mistral) as their responses can vary. Experiment with different phrasings and levels of detail to get the best results.

For defining agent roles and task plans within OpenManus, you will typically work with the configuration files (e.g., config.toml) or the Python code that defines your agent. Here's a conceptual example of how you might structure a task plan within OpenManus (the actual implementation will depend on the specific OpenManus project you are using):

```
# Example configuration for a web research agent
agent_name: WebResearcher
description: An agent that can perform web research and summarize findings.
llm_model: llama3 # Specify the Ollama model to use
tools:
  - name: WebBrowserTool
    config: {}
plan:
  - step: "Search the web for information on [topic]"
    tool: WebBrowserTool
    params:
      query: "[topic]"
  - step: "Summarize the top 3 search results"
    tool: LLMTool # A tool that sends a prompt to the LLM
    params:
      prompt: "Summarize the content of these web pages: [results from previous step]"
  - step: "Present the summary to the user"
    tool: OutputTool
    params:
      output: "[summary from previous step]"
```

This example shows a basic template for an agent that performs a web search, summarizes the results using an LLM, and then presents the summary. You can create more complex plans with multiple steps and different tools as needed for your specific automation tasks. By building up a library of effective prompts and agent templates, you can significantly accelerate the process of creating powerful and versatile AI agents with OpenManus and Ollama.

18. Community, GitHub Projects & Where to Contribute

The world of open-source AI is a vibrant and collaborative space. To further your journey with OpenManus and Ollama, engaging with the community and exploring the relevant GitHub projects is highly recommended.

Here are some key online communities where you can connect with other users, ask questions, and share your experiences:

- **Reddit:** Subreddits like /r/LocalLLaMA and /r/ollama are excellent places to find discussions, tutorials, and support related to running LLMs locally.
- **Ollama Discord Server:** The official Ollama project has a Discord server where you can get real-time help and chat with other users and developers.[29]

Key GitHub projects to explore include:

- **ollama/ollama** [29]: The main repository for the Ollama project. Here you can find the source code, documentation, and issue tracker.
- **mannaandpoem/OpenManus** [1]: One of the primary open-source initiatives aiming to replicate the capabilities of Manus AI.
- **henryalps/OpenManus** [2]: Another active OpenManus project with a focus on modularity and containerization.
- **rxyshww/OpenManus-node** [8]: A Node.js implementation of OpenManus.
- **open-webui/open-webui:** A user-friendly web interface for

interacting with Ollama, which can enhance your experience with local LLMs.

Contributing to these open-source projects is a fantastic way to learn, improve your skills, and help the community. Here are some ways you can contribute:

- **Reporting Issues:** If you encounter a bug or have a suggestion for a new feature, you can open an issue on the project's GitHub repository. Be as detailed as possible in your report.
- **Suggesting Features:** Share your ideas for how the projects can be improved or new functionalities that could be added.
- **Submitting Pull Requests:** If you have coding skills, you can contribute by fixing bugs or implementing new features and submitting your changes as a pull request.
- **Participating in Discussions:** Engage in discussions on the GitHub issue trackers, community forums, or Discord servers to help others and share your knowledge.
- **Writing Documentation:** Improving the documentation for these projects is always valuable and helps new users get started.

By actively participating in the open-source community, you can not only get support and learn from others but also contribute to the growth and evolution of these exciting technologies.

Referências citadas

1. How to Install & Run OpenManus Locally with Ollama – No API Keys Required, acessado em abril 2, 2025, https://dev.to/nodeshiftcloud/how-to-install-run-openmanus-locally-with-ollama-no-api-keys-required-2o4i
2. OpenManus is an open-source initiative to replicate the capabilities of the Manus AI agent, a state-of-the-art general-purpose AI developed by Monica, which excels in autonomously executing complex tasks. - GitHub, acessado em abril 2, 2025, https://github.com/henryalps/OpenManus
3. en.wikipedia.org, acessado em abril 2, 2025, https://

en.wikipedia.org/wiki/Manus_(AI_agent)#:~:text=Manus%20(hands%20in%20Latin)%20is,without%20direct%2Fcontinuous%20human%20guidance.

4. Manus (AI agent) - Wikipedia, acessado em abril 2, 2025, https://en.wikipedia.org/wiki/Manus_(AI_agent)

5. Manus AI: Revolutionizing Autonomy in Artificial Intelligence - OpenCV, acessado em abril 2, 2025, https://opencv.org/blog/manus-ai/

6. What is Manus AI?: The First General AI Agent Unveiled | by Tahir | Mar, 2025 | Medium, acessado em abril 2, 2025, https://medium.com/@tahirbalarabe2/what-is-manus-ai-the-first-general-ai-agent-unveiled-39a2c5702f91

7. Manus AI agent: how it works and real-world use cases, acessado em abril 2, 2025, https://blog.openreplay.com/manus-ai-agent-how-it-works-real-world-cases/

8. rxyshww/OpenManus-node - GitHub, acessado em abril 2, 2025, https://github.com/rxyshww/OpenManus-node

9. OpenManus: the Open-Source Alternative to Manus AI - Apidog, acessado em abril 2, 2025, https://apidog.com/blog/openmanus-open-source-manus-ai-alternative

10. OpenManus + Requesty: Your Gateway to 150+ Models, acessado em abril 2, 2025, https://www.requesty.ai/blog/openmanus-requesty-your-gateway-to-150-models

11. The Complete Guide to Building Your Free Local AI Assistant with Ollama and Open WebUI : r/selfhosted - Reddit, acessado em abril 2, 2025, https://www.reddit.com/r/selfhosted/comments/1jbk06h/the_complete_guide_to_building_your_free_local_ai/

12. After DeepSeek, Manus AI comes out of China: What is it and why is it making a buzz?, acessado em abril 2, 2025, https://www.indiatoday.in/technology/features/story/after-deepseek-manus-ai-comes-out-of-china-what-is-it-and-why-is-it-making-a-buzz-2691190-2025-03-09

13. What is Manus AI And How Does It Work? A Simple Explanation For Anyone - YouTube, acessado em abril 2, 2025, https://www.youtube.com/watch?v=eNZnAAEdhWo

14. China's Manus AI 'agent' could be our 1st glimpse at artificial ..., acessado em abril 2, 2025, https://www.livescience.com/technology/artificial-intelligence/chinas-manus-ai-agent-could-be-our-1st-glimpse-at-artificial-general-intelligence

15. Manus AI, Know the Use of General AI Agent, Capabilities & Examples - Great Learning, acessado em abril 2, 2025, https://www.mygreatlearning.com/blog/what-is-manus-ai/

16. Manus AI: The Best Autonomous AI Agent Redefining Automation and Productivity - Hugging Face, acessado em abril 2, 2025, https://huggingface.co/blog/LLMhacker/manus-ai-best-ai-agent

17. China's Manus AI Redefines Automation with Full Autonomy - FinTech Weekly, acessado em abril 2, 2025, https://www.fintechweekly.com/magazine/articles/chinese-monica-launches-manus-ai

18. OpenManus: A 3-Hour Replica of Manus, Now on GitHub with 3000+ Stars! - AIbase, acessado em abril 2, 2025, https://www.aibase.com/news/16066

19. Ollama | Mendix Glossary, acessado em abril 2, 2025, https://www.mendix.com/glossary/ollama/

20. Ollama - LangChain4j, acessado em abril 2, 2025, https://docs.langchain4j.dev/integrations/language-models/ollama/

21. What is Ollama? Introduction to the AI model management tool, acessado em abril 2, 2025, https://www.hostinger.com/tutorials/what-is-ollama

22. What is Ollama and how to use it: a quick guide [part 1] - Geshan's Blog, acessado em abril 2, 2025, https://geshan.com.np/blog/2025/02/what-is-ollama/

23. What is Ollama? Everything Important You Should Know - It's FOSS, acessado em abril 2, 2025, https://itsfoss.com/ollama/

24. Ollama: running Large Language Models locally - Andrea Grandi, acessado em abril 2, 2025, https://www.andreagrandi.it/posts/ollama-running-llm-locally/

25. Ollama: Easily run LLMs locally — Klu, acessado em abril 2, 2025, https://klu.ai/glossary/ollama

26. Ollama: How It Works Internally. Summary | by laiso - Medium, acessado em abril 2, 2025, https://medium.com/@laiso/ollama-under-the-hood-f8ed0f14d90c

27. Running local LLM with Ollama. Before starting let's understand how... | by Sanjeet Shukla | Feb, 2025 | Medium, acessado em abril 2, 2025, https://medium.com/@sanjeets1900/running-local-llm-with-ollama-02835fc97e98

28. Step-by-Step Guide: Running LLM Models with Ollama - DEV Community, acessado em abril 2, 2025, https://dev.to/snehalkadwe/how-to-setup-ollma-and-llm-4601

29. ollama/ollama: Get up and running with Llama 3.3 ... - GitHub, acessado em abril 2, 2025, https://github.com/ollama/ollama

30. Ollama Installation for macOS, Linux, and Windows - GitHub Pages, acessado em abril 2, 2025, https://translucentcomputing.github.io/kubert-assistant-lite/ollama.html

31. Run AI Models Locally: Ollama Tutorial (Step-by-Step Guide + WebUI) - YouTube, acessado em abril 2, 2025, https://www.youtube.com/watch?v=Lb5D892-2HY

32. Guide to Installing and Locally Running Ollama LLM models in Comfy (ELI5 Level) - Reddit, acessado em abril 2, 2025, https://www.reddit.com/r/ollama/comments/1ibhxvm/guide_to_installing_and_locally_running_ollama/

33. Run Gemma with Ollama | Google AI for Developers - Gemini API, acessado em abril 2, 2025, https://ai.google.dev/gemma/docs/integrations/ollama

34. Gemma 3 + Ollama on Colab: A Developer's Quickstart | by E. Huizenga | Google Cloud, acessado em abril 2, 2025, https://medium.com/google-cloud/gemma-3-ollama-on-colab-a-developers-quickstart-7bbf93ab8fef

35. A Step-by-Step Guide to Install Gemma-3 Locally with Ollama or Transformers, acessado em abril 2, 2025, https://

dev.to/nodeshiftcloud/a-step-by-step-guide-to-install-gemma-3-locally-with-ollama-or-transformers-12g6

36. How to Set Up and Run Gemma 3 Locally With Ollama - DataCamp, acessado em abril 2, 2025, https://www.datacamp.com/tutorial/gemma-3-ollama

37. How to Run Llama 3 Locally - Codecademy, acessado em abril 2, 2025, https://www.codecademy.com/article/run-llama-3-locally

38. Unlocking LLaMA 3 with Ollama: A Beginner's Guide tutorial - Lablab.ai, acessado em abril 2, 2025, https://lablab.ai/t/llama3-with-ollama

39. How to Set Up and Run Llama 3 Locally With Ollama and GPT4ALL - DataCamp, acessado em abril 2, 2025, https://www.datacamp.com/tutorial/run-llama-3-locally

40. Run Llama 3 Locally with Ollama - Medium, acessado em abril 2, 2025, https://medium.com/@manuelescobar-dev/running-llama-3-locally-with-ollama-9881706df7ac

41. How to run Mistral using Ollama - GPU Mart, acessado em abril 2, 2025, https://www.gpu-mart.com/blog/how-to-run-mistral-using-ollama

42. Ollama Install Mistral Guide | Restackio, acessado em abril 2, 2025, https://www.restack.io/p/ollama-install-answer-mistral-cat-ai

43. How to Run Mistral Small 3.1 Locally Using Ollama: A Step-by-Step Guide - Apidog, acessado em abril 2, 2025, https://apidog.com/blog/run-mistral-small-3-1-locally-ollama/

44. Mistral 7B LLM: Run Locally with Ollama | by Parmar shyamsinh | Medium, acessado em abril 2, 2025, https://medium.com/@parmarshyamsinh/mistral-7b-llm-run-locally-with-ollama-bf10494be857

45. Running Ollama on a Raspberry Pi - I am Bill Meyer, acessado em abril 2, 2025, https://iambillmeyer.com/posts/2025-01-01-ollama-on-raspberry-pi/

46. Beginner's Guide to Installing Openmanus, acessado em abril 2, 2025, https://www.oneclickitsolution.com/

centerofexcellence/aiml/openmanus-setup-guide

47. OpenManus vs. RPA | How AI Agents Are Revolutionizing Automation, acessado em abril 2, 2025, https://www.oneclickitsolution.com/ centerofexcellence/aiml/openmanus-research-automation

48. Breaking Free from AI Waitlists: How OpenManus is Changing the Game for Developers | by Sebastian Petrus | Mar, 2025 | Medium, acessado em abril 2, 2025, https:// medium.com/@sebastian-petrus/how-openmanus- changing-developers-game-862e5ab44a70

49. Integrate Open MANUS on Open Web UI: Enhancing Automation & User Experience #11574 - GitHub, acessado em abril 2, 2025, https://github.com/open-webui/open-webui/ discussions/11574

50. Code Explanation: "OpenManus: An Autonomous Agent Platform" - DEV Community, acessado em abril 2, 2025, https://dev.to/foxgem/openmanus-an-autonomous-agent- platform-8nl

51. Breaking Free from AI Waitlists: How OpenManus is Changing the Game for Developers, acessado em abril 2, 2025, https://sebastian-petrus.medium.com/how- openmanus-changing-developers-game-862e5ab44a70

52. OpenManus: the Open-Source Alternative to Manus AI - Apidog, acessado em abril 2, 2025, https://apidog.com/ blog/openmanus-open-source-manus-ai-alternative/

53. README.md - mannaandpoem/OpenManus - GitHub, acessado em abril 2, 2025, https://github.com/ mannaandpoem/OpenManus/blob/main/README.md

54. Ollama LLM - AnythingLLM Docs, acessado em abril 2, 2025, https://docs.useanything.com/setup/llm- configuration/local/ollama

55. Made a ManusAI alternative that run locally : r/LocalLLaMA - Reddit, acessado em abril 2, 2025, https:// www.reddit.com/r/LocalLLaMA/comments/1jbwk65/ made_a_manusai_alternative_that_run_locally/

56. Hello World to Open Manus and Browser-use: AI Web

Automation | by Xin Cheng - Medium, acessado em abril 2, 2025, https://medium.com/@billtcheng2013/hello-world-to-open-manus-and-browser-use-ai-web-automation-d74b0f7a9448

57. Exploring Manus AI Agent. Autonomous AI Revolution and How to Get... | by Naveen Krishnan | Mar, 2025 | Towards AI, acessado em abril 2, 2025, https://pub.towardsai.net/exploring-manus-ai-agent-2e1e168aa4d6

58. Build an AI-Powered Technical Analysis Stock Dashboard in Python with Streamlit and Ollama - Substack, acessado em abril 2, 2025, https://substack.com/home/post/p-155192095?utm_campaign=post&utm_medium=web

59. Manus AI:: (What It Is, Features, Usecases, Price, Alternatives, How To Access) - AI Mode, acessado em abril 2, 2025, https://aimode.co/app/manus/

60. Everything You Need to Know About Manus AI: Features, Access, and Use Cases - Kanerika, acessado em abril 2, 2025, https://kanerika.com/blogs/manus-ai/

61. What is Manus AI and How It Transforms Automation - PageOn.ai, acessado em abril 2, 2025, https://www.pageon.ai/blog/manus-ai

62. OpenManus AI Agent Tutorial: Build & Deploy in 15 Minutes (No Coding Required!), acessado em abril 2, 2025, https://www.youtube.com/watch?v=oayv1ah6-4M

63. Build your own voice assistant and run it locally: Whisper + Ollama + Bark | by Duy Huynh, acessado em abril 2, 2025, https://medium.com/@vndee.huynh/build-your-own-voice-assistant-and-run-it-locally-whisper-ollama-bark-c80e6f815cba

64. A local AI Voice Assistant using Granite-7B, Ollama, InstructLab and AlwaysReddy, acessado em abril 2, 2025, https://www.youtube.com/watch?v=inlada3SiNA

65. Ollama Fundamentals 01 - Your Own AI Assistant Running Locally - YouTube, acessado em abril 2, 2025, https://www.youtube.com/watch?v=Lxb_cgLkOHU

66. Build a Meta Llamma-3 Powered Voice Assistant with

Ollama and Python - YouTube, acessado em abril 2, 2025, https://m.youtube.com/watch?v=X8rpOSKDg6I

67. Building a Sandboxed Environment for AI generated Code Execution | by Anukriti Ranjan, acessado em abril 2, 2025, https://anukriti-ranjan.medium.com/building-a-sandboxed-environment-for-ai-generated-code-execution-e1351301268a

68. Sandboxing Agentic AI Workflows with WebAssembly | NVIDIA Technical Blog, acessado em abril 2, 2025, https://developer.nvidia.com/blog/sandboxing-agentic-ai-workflows-with-webassembly/

69. substratusai/sandboxai: Run AI generated code in isolated sandboxes - GitHub, acessado em abril 2, 2025, https://github.com/substratusai/sandboxai

70. Run AI-Generated Code Safely with Daytona Sandboxes, acessado em abril 2, 2025, https://www.daytona.io/dotfiles/run-ai-generated-code-safely-with-daytona-sandboxes-part-1

71. How to Install Deepseek on Raspberry Pi: A Step-by-Step Guide - OneClick IT Consultancy, acessado em abril 2, 2025, https://www.oneclickitsolution.com/centerofexcellence/aiml/install-deepseek-raspberry-pi-guide

72. Running DeepSeek R1 Locally on a Raspberry Pi - DEV Community, acessado em abril 2, 2025, https://dev.to/jeremycmorgan/running-deepseek-r1-locally-on-a-raspberry-pi-1gh8

73. OpenManus Installation in Ubuntu 22.04 - YouTube, acessado em abril 2, 2025, https://www.youtube.com/watch?v=62YmIsZzz3M

74. Raspberry Pi Orchestration : 8 Steps - Instructables, acessado em abril 2, 2025, https://www.instructables.com/Raspberry-Pi-orchestration/

75. Running ollama with Llama3.2:3b on a Raspberry Pi 5 8 Gig - runs, but "unimportable"?, acessado em abril 2, 2025, https://www.reddit.com/r/ollama/comments/1ievb8g/running_ollama_with_llama323b_on_a_raspberry_pi_5/

76. Running Ollama on the Raspberry Pi - Pi My Life Up, acessado em abril 2, 2025, https://pimylifeup.com/raspberry-pi-ollama/

77. Ollama GUI: ChatGPT but offline and private and it runs on Raspberry Pi 5 8GB, acessado em abril 2, 2025, https://forums.raspberrypi.com/viewtopic.php?t=383314

78. How to Run LLMs Locally on Raspberry Pi Using Ollama AI - It's FOSS, acessado em abril 2, 2025, https://itsfoss.com/raspberry-pi-ollama-ai-setup/

79. Build Multi-Agent AI System with OpenAI Swarm using Ollama - NodeShift, acessado em abril 2, 2025, https://nodeshift.com/blog/build-multi-agent-ai-system-with-openai-swarm-using-ollama

80. VS Code integration — Nextflow documentation, acessado em abril 2, 2025, https://nextflow.io/docs/latest/vscode.html

81. Ollama - LangChain, acessado em abril 2, 2025, https://python.langchain.com/v0.1/docs/integrations/providers/ollama/

82. How to Use MCP with Ollama (without Claude, with Dolphin MCP) - Apidog, acessado em abril 2, 2025, https://apidog.com/blog/mcp-ollama